FATUS GITOSA~~URUS~~

Mogul

&

CLYDE

Take That Books is an imprint of
Take That Ltd.
P.O.Box 200
Harrogate
HG1 4XB

Copyright © 1993 Take That Books

10 9 8 7 6 5 4 3 2 1

ISBN 1-873668-15-5

Layout, illustrations and typesetting by Impact Design, P.O.Box 200, Harrogate, HG1 4XB.

Printed and bound in Great Britain.

TAKE THAT BOOKS

The Hackodon (*Tabloidia Scumii*)

Habitat: Behind bushes or peering over walls.

Identification: Usually found in packs. Never without a camera, tape-recorder and notebook.

Food: Scandal, revelations and exclusives.

Behaviour: Spends entire life hassling its victims in search of incriminating evidence of perceived misdoings. Invents 'details' if real facts are not interesting enough. Has a total disregard for any form of privacy. Spends as much time making up expense claims as writing stories.

The Anorakasurus
(Trainia Spotta)

Habitat: The end of train platforms.
Identification: Anorak, jeans, woolly jumper and trainers.
Food: New numbers and unusual rolling stock movements.
Behaviour: Sits for hours scribbling into a small school exercise book. Only stops to wipe spectacles with a snotty rag, and to take a sip of hot chocolate from a flask. Also likes reading dirty mags and looking over next-door's fence when they are in the bath.

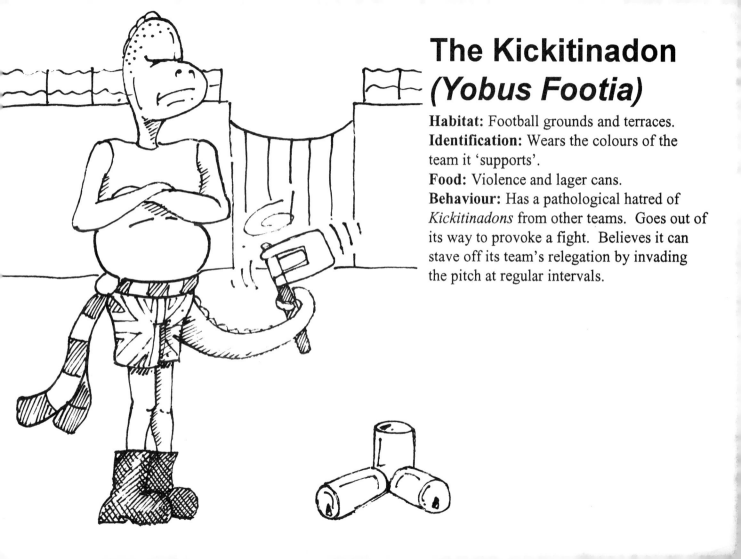

The Kickitinadon
(Yobus Footia)

Habitat: Football grounds and terraces.
Identification: Wears the colours of the team it 'supports'.
Food: Violence and lager cans.
Behaviour: Has a pathological hatred of *Kickitinadons* from other teams. Goes out of its way to provoke a fight. Believes it can stave off its team's relegation by invading the pitch at regular intervals.

The Jogadon
(Puffa Panta)

Habitat: City parks and fun runs.
Identification: Latest designer clothing, with top-of-the-range running shoes. Fetid running socks.
Food: P.B.s and tin medals.
Behaviour: Bores everyone stupid talking about times and personal bests. Has an impressive list of excuses for not running well. Believes that it is the fittest animal ever to roam the earth. Liberally spreads petroleum jelly on its crotch.

The Lollypoposaur
(Crossa Nowii)

Habitat: Middle of roads.
Identification: Big white coat and the biggest lollipop you've ever seen.
Food: Wine gums and toffees.
Behaviour: Likes stepping out in front of cars. Carries a cardboard sign for fending off oncoming articulated lorries. Very kind to children. Difficult to spot on Zebra-crossings.

The Firstaidadon (*Sint Joanas*)

Habitat: Local sporting events.
Identification: Carries a large bag of bandages.
Food: Deep cuts and broken bones.
Behaviour: Treats every minor accident as a 'life threat' situation. Goes over the top on bandaging everything that moves. Favourite battle cry is "Let him get some air"

The Reguleras *(Barstool Hogus)*

Habitat: At or near the bar.
Identification: Greeted with a pint when it walks into the local pub.
Food: A pint of usual.
Behaviour: Knows everybody by name and talks about how things used to be.

Blottotops *(Dino Nonerectum)*

Habitat: Pub floors.
Identification: Either staggering or horizontal.
Food: Beer, lager and shorts.
Behaviour: Drinks until it falls down.

The Secretaromus
(Ofis Receptus)

Habitat: Reception desks and switchboards.
Identification: Bimboid appearance used to put Clientosaurs and Reposaurs at ease.
Food: Gossip, memos and chocolate bars.
Behaviour: Looks good but doesn't really do much. Spends a long time on the phone to friends and can often be seen painting finger talons.

Fatus Gitosaurus (*Lazium Sloberdosa*)

Habitat: Favourite armchair and the local pub.
Identification: Knotted hanky on head and cigarette hanging out from side of mouth.
Food: Junk food and cooking of Erindaurus.
Behaviour: Only ever looks after number one. Hates house work and all other dinosaurs, especially if they don't come from his swamp. Walks into the house with dirty boots on. Has an unhealthy desire for fast cars and young female dinosaurs about half his age. Believes he can still do everything he did at age 18.

Erindaurus
(Trublus Strifus)

Habitat: In the vicinity of the kitchen sink.
Identification: Wears curlers and carries a rolling-pin
Food: Own cooking and junk food brought home by
the Fatus Gitosaurus.
Behaviour: Talks... and talks... and talks... and talks...
Never short of anything to nag about. Obsessed with
tidying up and often removes Fatus' possessions so he
can't find them. Always wants to watch Soaps when
the football is on the telly.

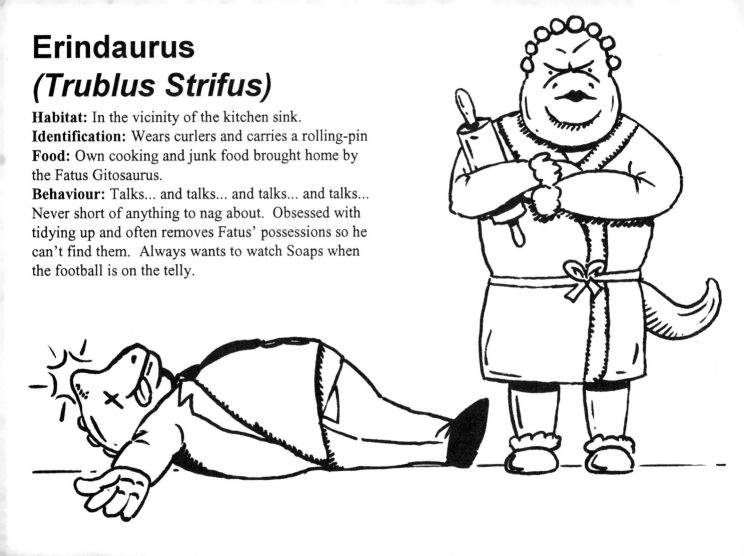

The Bratosaur
(Pestus Konstantus)

Habitat: Under the feet of the Parentosaur.
Identification: Can usually be found doing anything it is not allowed to do.
Food: Sweets, chocolate and fizzy drinks.
Behaviour: Creates havoc wherever it treads, drives the Parentosaur to distraction, but avoids punishment with its cute smile.

The Commutosis
(Layt Yetagenus)

Habitat: Train platforms, banks and offices.
Identification: Pinstripe suit, briefcase and frustrated appearance.
Food: Sandwiches, mints and strong coffee.
Behaviour: Never looks at other Commutosi, stares at newspapers with regular glances at watch.

Bee-Arodon
(Crapposervix)

Habitat: Dirty station platforms.
Identification: Can be found arriving very late into its habitat, due to gigantic Jurassic leaves being in its way.
Food: Tickets, passes and Commutosi.
Behaviour: Charges a fortune for substandard service and never sticks to its predicted running schedule.

The Bumcrakodon
(Trousa Slipera)

Habitat: Holes in the ground.
Identification: Trousers falling down to reveal expanses of white flesh.
Food: Chips and tea.
Behaviour: Takes regular breaks when it can be seen leaning on shovel and wolf-whistling at the passing Bimbosaurs.

The Bossobaur
(Slavedrivus Rex)

Habitat: Never leaves the office.
Identification: Premature greying of hair, reddish hide from high blood pressure, growls continuously.
Food: Business lunches, French wines and fat cigars.
Behaviour: Never satisfied with anything, obscene craving for wealth, cannot understand failing of subservient Workosaurs.

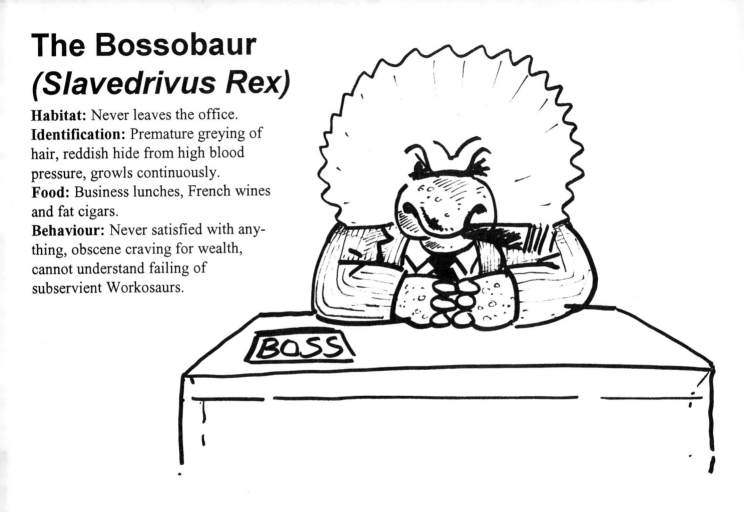

The Revosaurus
(Moretea Vica)

Habitat: Small parishes and pulpits.
Identification: Wears a Woofasaur collar and carries a cup of tea.
Food: Wine and bread.
Behaviour: Kindly nature, and strong belief that everything which happens is for the better. Can put an entire Congregatiodon to sleep with one sermon.

The Ticketodon
(Gotcha Matus)

Habitat: City pavements and car parks.
Identification: Related to the Clamponoid. Can be seen memorising car number plates and making notes of times.
Food: Anything that's only been there ''a couple of minutes''.
Behaviour: Places small pieces of paper on victims' car windscreens. A masochistic beast, totally immune to any form of pleading. Hated by most other dinosaurs who would gladly shove the Ticketodon's head up their exhaust pipe.

NO PARKING

The Vacuasaur
(Sucka Stronga)

Habitat: Under the stairs.
Identification: Can be upright with attachments, or horizontal with a long snout.
Food: Dirt, dust and small valuables.
Behaviour: Refuses to clean properly unless emptied regularly. Can't reach the edges despite maker's claims. Uncanny knack of taking items it is not supposed to.

The Caravanica
(Highway Cloggus)

Habitat: Small country lanes.

Identification: At the head of a huge queue of traffic. Usually pulled by a vehicle with woefully inadequate power.

Food: Tourist traps and beauty spots.

Behaviour: Only appears during fine weather and bank holidays. Totally selfish. Displays a single-minded disregard for all other road users, and can't understand why the 115 miles of traffic behind him is getting hot under the collar. Often travels in packs to make it even more difficult for overtaking. Usually called 'George', wears a flat cap and smokes a pipe.

The Shellsuitinite
(Gaudi Culoura)

Habitat: Sports club bars and airport terminals.

Identification: Bright, striking colours. Rustling noise on movement.

Food: Anything posey.

Behaviour: Slinks around trying to impress with everything it owns, and usually fails. Does a good impression of being 'the oldest swinger in town'. Last read a fashion magazine in 1956 because it had a good article on crepe soles.

Grandmadea
(Oldus Cogerii Regina)

Habitat: Coffee mornings and bridge parties.
Identification: Can usually be found hovering around the younger family, in particular *The Bratosaurus*.
Food: Earl Grey and sponge cake.
Behaviour: Kindly nature. Seems obsessed with knitting more jumpers than anybody can wear. Spends a lot of time trying to make everything just perfect, and nagging *The Grandpadea*.

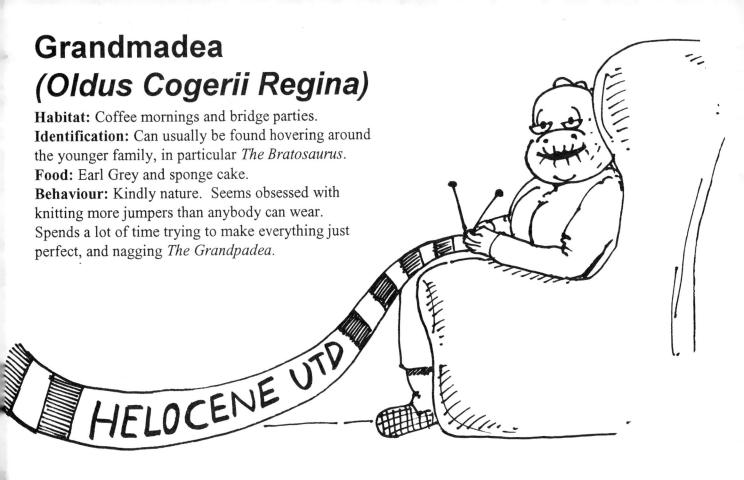

HELOCENE UTD

Grandpadea
(Oldus Cogerii Rex)

Habitat: Gardens, allotments and favourite armchair.

Identification: Shuffles around with the aid of a stick. Still keeps ration card in back pocket.

Food: Black tea and extra strong mints.

Behaviour: Kindly nature. Talks a lot about 'The Good Old Days' and what it was like during the war. Spends most of time in the garden, hiding from *The Grandmadea*.

The Heavasaurus
(Yawnus Vomita)

Habitat: The streets.
Identification: Can be seen leaning against lampposts and walls after closing time.
Food: Diced carrots.
Behaviour: Staggers in random directions, stares intensely at the floor and then covers the pavement with that evenings consumption. Employed by the local Chinese restaurant to display its menu around town.

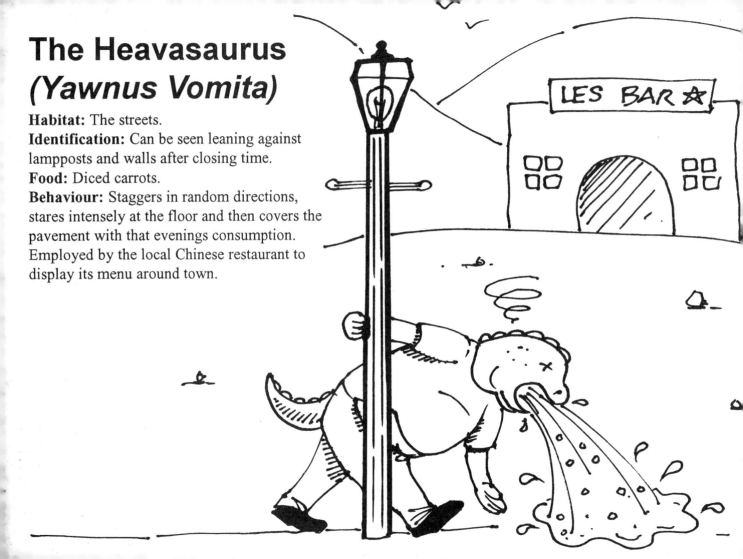

LES BAR

The Umpirodor
(Howizee Howizee)

Habitat: Small village cricket pitches.
Identification: White coat, eleven jumpers round waist and glum expression.
Food: Loud appeals and cream teas.
Behaviour: Waddles around behind the wickets, never responds to appeals but raises index finger when least expected. Would call play off because of bad light even if the match was taking place on the Sun.

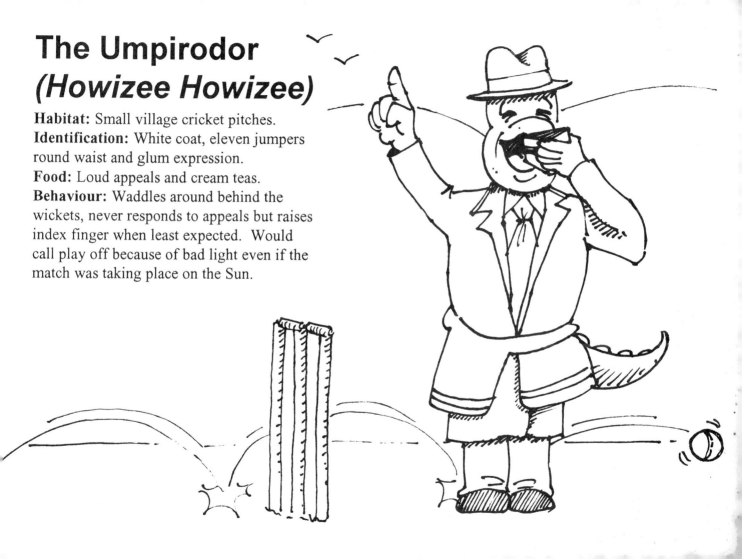

The Golfobore
(Handicapia Greatus)

Habitat: The nineteenth hole.
Identification: Looks out at the course but never leaves the bar stool.
Food: Best bitter and free peanuts.
Behaviour: Talks a good round, but has never been seen with a club in the hand. Bores everyone else stupid with memories of its 'hole in one' from 346 yards back in 1953. Claims that it can remember every shot it has ever taken.

The Woofosaur (K9)

Habitat: Close to lampposts and in front of the fire.
Identification: Four legs, fleas and collar.
Food: Slippers and cats.
Behaviour: Pretends to be ''man's best friend'', but always insists on going for a walk in the worst weather.

The Ownadogs (Walkees Walkees)

Habitat: Plodding forlornly along wet streets and alleys.
Identification: Can be found at the other end of the lead to *The Woofosaur*.
Food: Newspapers and cans of beer.
Behaviour: Takes *The Woofosaur* for walks to the local pub and back. Occasionally throws a stick as far away as possible, expecting it to be 'fetched'.

The Photokopiadon
(Calle Engineerex)

Habitat: Offices and workplaces.
Identification: Buff coloured plastic, one metre high, two flaps
in open position, Engineer with toolbox poking around inside.
Food: Paper, important documents and engineers.
Behaviour: Defecates paper with low whirring sound,
usually only works for one person
in the entire office.

The Strikosaur
(Picketum Picketum)

Habitat: Outside factory gates.
Identification: Carries placards and Union banners.
Food: Anti-company propaganda.
Behaviour: Shouts abuse at anyone going through the gates. Hasn't much idea why it is striking, but it's bound to be good for the 'werkers'. Favourite word is 'Scab', but it couldn't tell you what it means.

NO TO HELOCENE BLACK LEGS

Handlebaronchops
(Skwadron Leadon)

Habitat: Conservative clubs.
Identification: Large handlebar moustache and monocle.
Food: Anything so long as it's British.
Behaviour: Can't believe how the country is going to the dogs. Challenges young dinosaurs about their dress; nobody would look like that in his day.

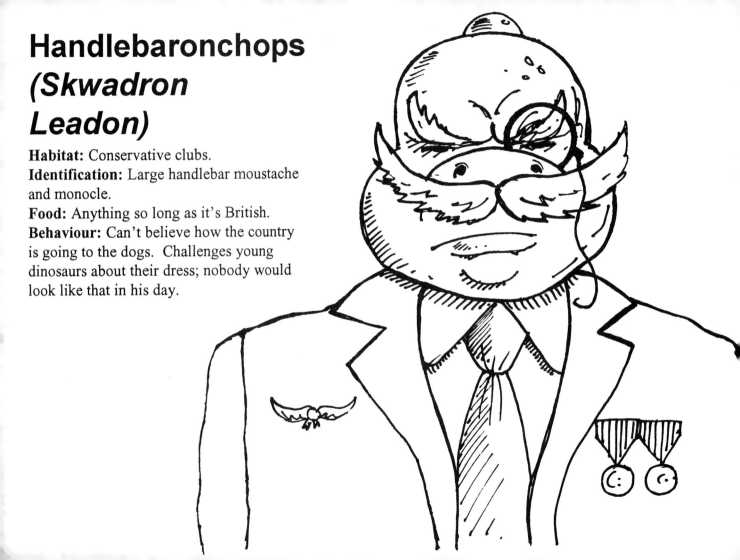

The Fisheranth
(Thisa Bigga)

Habitat: Quays, piers and river banks.
Identification: Hat full of hooks and long boots.
Food: Flies, worms and maggots.
Behaviour: Stretches arms as wide as they'll go and exaggerates about the size of the tiddler that got away.

The Dinofax
(Filo Yuppia)

Habitat: The tops of tables in full view of everybody.

Identification: Leather bound and stuffed with an unnecessary amount of rubbish.

Food: Paper and plastic bits.

Behaviour: Parasite of the Yuppisaurus. Tries to convey importance on its host.

The Citusgentosaur
(Bowler Bowler)

Habitat: Financial areas of the city.
Identification: Bowler hat, pinstripe suit
and briefcase. All Citusgentosaurs are
identical and act like clones of one another.
Food: Sandwiches found in briefcase along
with a copy of 'Big Busts Monthly'.
Behaviour: Likes to tell other dinosaurs
how important he is. Mutters indecipherable
rubbish about the need for Total Quality
Management. Has never had an original
thought. Keeps its nose in the proximity of
its boss' backside.

The Guardum Securiarch (*Morethanme Jobsworthica*)

Habitat: Anywhere that doesn't really need guarding.

Identification: Sits behind a real or imagined barrier and proudly displays uniform.

Food: Passes, permits and dockets.

Behaviour: Officious nature. Doesn't let anybody do anything without a piece of paper. Takes great pleasure in being as obstructive as possible. Doesn't recognise any other dinosaurs without an identity card, even though he has seen them every day for the past 20 years.

The Armcharites
(Fatus Situs)

Habitat: Corners of the living room.
Identification: Similar to the *Fatus
Gitosaurus* but with a well worn area on
its backside and square eyes.
Food: Cans of lager and cheeseburgers.
Behaviour: Only moves to switch over
channels. Can remember the start times
of football programmes but little else.

The Reposaur
(Dooya Adealia)

Habitat: On the road most of the time, or waiting in reception lobbies.

Identification: Too much make-up or after-shave. Always carries a suitcase full of samples.

Food: The gullible.

Behaviour: Slimey approach, refuses to take 'no' as an answer. Always seems to be selling something of which you have plenty. Has iron feet for sticking in the door when you try and close it.

The Clamponoid
(Gotcha Wheelsa)

Habitat: White, unmarked vans and offices miles from anywhere.

Identification: Can be seen hovering near yellow lines and private car parks.

Food: Car tyres and bodywork.

Behaviour: Recklessly attaches metal clamps to victims' cars, makes them travel miles to pay for the removal, and then clamps them again before they return.

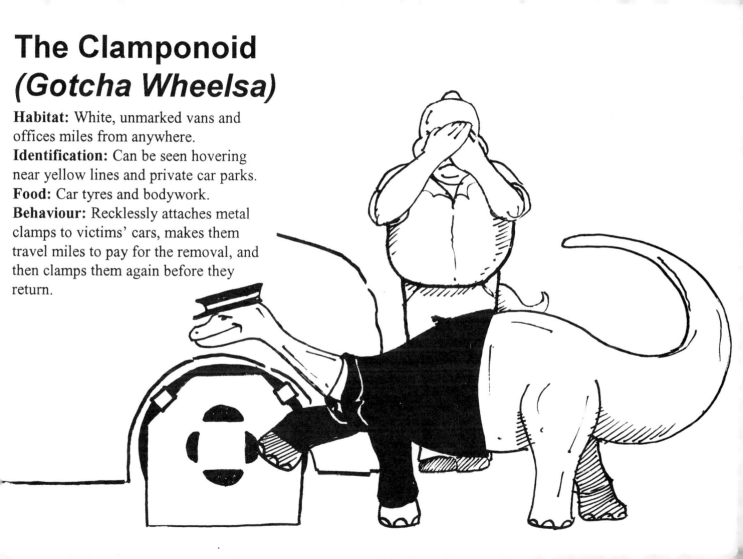

The Wreckasella
(Banga Dodgyus)

Habitat: Second-hand car forecourts.
Identification: Gold chains, large watches and cockney accents.
Food: Clocked cars, blank MOT certificates and false plates.
Behaviour: Somehow manages to have the best vehicles ever built sitting on their forecourt waiting for you to buy them. Pick any mileage you want - all on the same vehicle!

HONEST PTERRY

The Geldorfotops
(Popstarus Agingus)

Habitat: Television appeals and charity dinners.
Identification: Career's on the way down which needs a media boost.
Food: Earthquakes, famines and human rights infringements.
Behaviour: 'Spontaneously' comes out of the woodwork when there is food around. Performs for 'free' to raise money. And then there's all that TV exposure....

The Nodding Sabresaur
(K9 Upndownis)

Habitat: Car dashboards.

Identification: Nods its head when car goes over bumps.

Food: Nodding dog biscuits and nodding water.

Behaviour: Nods in agreement with the furry dice, 'John and Tracy' sun-visors and the Christmas tree shaped smelly thing.

The Checkoutagil
(Barcowd Reeda)

Habitat: Check-out desks in supermarkets.
Identification: Sits behind the till, armed with a barcode reader which only works 20% of the time.
Food: Chewing-gum and crisps.
Behaviour: Stares gormlessly into space and occasionally utters ''next bane of my life, please''. Tendency to over-ring unless you can decipher the hieroglyphics on the till receipt. Has a reputation as a 'bit of a go-er' and 'knows' most of the lads in her street. Lets her mates take goods from the shop without ringing them through.

The Bloodsukador
(Bankus Managerus)

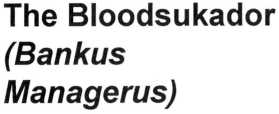

Habitat: Plush offices in banks.
Identification: Drives a Rolls-Royce, and holidays in the Caymen Islands.
Food: Bank charges, interest and collateral.
Behaviour: Takes your money, refuses to give it back, acts with death-defying arrogance and forecloses on loans when you least expect it. Has no qualms about lending money to third-world despots and dodgy property companies. Likes to see its clients squirm. Takes great pleasure in seeing widows and orphans sent to the workhouse.

The Lugodon
(Princeo Wayles)

Habitat: Buckingham Palace and Higrove House.

Identification: Two wing-like protrusions on either side of head.

Food: That fit for a King.

Behaviour: Despite being rather stupid, the Lugodon likes to assert its views on all subjects especially architecture. Plays the game of the masses known as 'Polo'. Appears to be very friendly with The *Hackodons* who feature him regularly in their tabloid newspapers. Somehow manages to marry attractive *Erindaurs*, but then deserts them. Mothered by a wise *Queenadon* who is clinging to her throne in order to save the rest of the modern dinosaur kingdom from the *Lugodon*'s opinions.

The Postus Ofisaurus
(Longa Queix)

Habitat: Town centres and large estates.
Identification: Red sign, small narrow holes in walls, shut when needed, often long queues snaking out of the door.
Food: Letters, parcels and pension books.
Behaviour: Non-smiling service, imitates petty officialdom, only one window open at lunch times.

The Snookotops
(Pota Blackun)

Habitat: Private snooker clubs.
Identification: Wears a waistcoat and bow-tie, but doesn't serve food.
Food: Glasses of water.
Behaviour: Paces round and round a green baize table, stoops down at regular intervals and closes one eye. Spends a lot of time in Sheffield. Prefers cups of tea to sex.

Werkus Clubadon
(Passa Resolution)

Habitat: Smoky halls.
Identification: Flat caps and accompanied by whippets.
Food: Beer and skittles.
Behaviour: All actions are governed by 'The Committee'.

The Yuppieasaur (*Richum Parentos*)

Habitat: Wine bars and flash cabriolet sports cars.

Identification: Red braces, striped shirts and baggy trousers. Distinctive ''Ya, Ya, Ya'' call.

Food: Champagne and caviar.

Behaviour: All Yuppieasaurs are 'something' in the city, but don't really understand what it is they are supposed to be doing. Likes to be seen spending money, most of which has been magically acquired from dealing with inside information. The rest of the money comes from 'daddy'.

The Ticketinspectatops
(Anymorfares)

Habitat: Trains and buses.

Identification: Carries a ticket punch and a large timetable.

Food: Excess fares.

Behaviour: Takes everybody's tickets and puts holes in them. Loves nothing better than a dinosaur travelling outside of the stipulated hours on the ticket. Has an ability to memorise thousands of permutations and combination of fares. Any leniency is deemed "More than me job's worth."

The Taxitops
(Whertoo Guvnor)

Habitat: Black cabs and other carriages.
Identification: Illuminates a miniature sign when 'for hire'.
Food: Fares, gossip and large banknotes with no change (known as optional tips).
Behaviour: Likes to throw its passengers around the cab with lurchy driving, and talk non-stop about who it gave a lift to "earlier in the day". All *Taxitops* are football specialists awaiting the call to manage the national side, and experts on politics and the economy. Refuses to go South of the River at night.

The Chauffeursaur
(Drivon Jamesus)

Habitat: The driving seats of long black cars.
Identification: Peeked cap and dark uniform.
Food: Directions from the boss.
Behaviour: Drives from one end of the country to the other while its boss does the mail and makes calls on the portable phone. Steadfastly ignores all business details discussed in the vehicle. Likes to polish the car and hates birds.

The Dictatorsaurus Rex
(Throwum Injailes)

Habitat: South American and African states.
Identification: Wears an infeasibly large collection of medals from wars that never took place.
Food: Political opponents.
Behaviour: Dangerous. Loves to abuse human rights and make people disappear. Not recognised by most governments, but that doesn't stop them supplying arms to the Dictatorsaurus.

The Newsiceras (*Depressum Depressum*)

Habitat: TV news studios.
Identification: Never changing dead-pan look.
Food: Death, destruction and murder stories.
Behaviour: Informs all other dinosaurs about how unpleasant the world is. Likes to throw in a humorous ditty at the end of the newscast. Most *Newsicerases* write books about their strange hobbies to take advantage of their media fame.

...amikus
(Weatheris Badus)

Habitat: Stands in front of big maps.
Identification: Wears an obscenely bright tie.
Food: Floods, droughts and hurricanes.
Behaviour: Waves its hands around while talking about the weather. Rarely gets anything right. Blamed by most of the dinosaur population for the rain.

Habitat: Allotments and ho...
Identification: Green fingers.
Food: Perennials, annuals and hardy an...
Behaviour: Likes to dig holes and fill them again with greenery. Looks continuously from the ground to the sky and back again. Spends more time worrying about the parish flower show than world peace.

The Fumasaur
(Pipa Smoka)

Habitat: Pubs, restaurants and public transport.
Identification: Clay protrusion from mouth.
Food: Tobacco.
Behaviour: Wrongly believes that all other dinosaurs like the smell of pipe smoke. Can clear a restaurant in seconds. Needs to re-light the pipe every three seconds and push a little white fluffy stick into it. Always wears a colourful woolly cardigan.

Neighbaurs
(Knowsey Buggas)

Habitat: Next door to you.
Identification: Moving net curtains
Food: Gossip about the Jones's
Behaviour: Always tries to go one better than you. Insists that you stay as quiet as a Doormausasaur while it creates as much noise as possible. Knows everything that's going-on in the street, but misses the thieves ransacking your house.

The Teachiadon (Lecturum Ad Nausium)

Habitat: Schools, colleges and universities.

Identification: Rarely seen face-on. Unkempt hair and bad breath.

Food: Homework.

Behaviour: Usually has back to class, writing never-ending formulae on the black-board. Can kill at 300 yards with a piece of chalk. Takes extraordinarily long holidays and claims to be over-worked. Occasionally makes an effort when trying to bed over-eager female students.

The Insuradon (*Financia Advisia*)

Habitat: In every bank, building society, insurance house and estate agency.

Identification: Bears a logo to 'prove' it is independent.

Food: Redundancy payments and family inheritances.

Behaviour: Untrained salesmen who know nothing about finance. Only concerned about their commission, and will give any advice necessary to close the sale. Never independent. Changes job regularly. More likely to retire to Bermuda with your money than give you a good rate of return.

The Latestops
(Incomprehensibleshouta)

Habitat: On street corners and outside railway stations.
Identification: Shouts loud and totally indecipherable words into your ear when you pass the stall.
Food: Newspapers and magazines.
Behaviour: Appears with a glum face in all weathers. Announces different headlines with the same shout every day. Picks nose when bored and refuses to tell you the time when asked.

Minertors
(Digus Deepus)

Habitat: Dark, dirty, underground tunnels.
Identification: Black faces with white around eyes and mouth, similar to a *Pandadon*.
Food: Coal, gold and diamonds.
Behaviour: Disappears underground for long periods every day in a small cage. When not digging, *Minertors* like to join picket lines. Not many left, nearing extinction at the hands of the *Torysaurs*.

The Rambosaur (Blastem Blastem)

Habitat: Big budget Hollywood movies.
Identification: Infeasibly large weapons bristling from every orifice.
Food: Death and destruction.
Behaviour: Pretends to be the downtrodden hero who comes good and blasts the commie-scum to hell. Brain the size of a pea and even smaller genitalia.

The Postielets
(Patancat)

Habitat: Old red bicycles.

Identification: Struggles around with huge sack of mail in all weathers. Followed by a black and white cat.

Food: Letters, stamps and postcodes.

Behaviour: Always seems to know more about what's going on in your household than you do. Can fold anything with 'Do Not Bend' on the envelope. Plays football with poorly wrapped parcels in the sorting office.

MORE HUMOUR TITLES...

The Ancient Art of Farting by Dr. C.Huff
Ever since time began, man (not woman) has farted. Does this ability lie behind many of the so far unexplained mysteries of history ? You Bet - because Dr. C.Huff's research shows conclusively there's something rotten about history taught in schools. If you do most of your reading on the throne, then this book is your ideal companion. Sit back and fart yourself silly as you split your sides laughing! *£3.99*

The Hangover Handbook & Boozer's Bible
(in the shape of a beercan)
Ever groaned, burped and cursed the morning after, as Vesuvius erupted in your stomach, a bass drummer thumped on your brain and a canary fouled its nest in your throat? Then you need these 100+ hangover remedies. There's an exclusive Hangover Ratings Chart, a Boozer's Calendar, a Hangover Clinic, and you can meet the Great Drunks of History, try the Boozer's Reading Chart, etc., etc. *£3.99*

The Elvis Spotter's Guide
Strange inconsistencies behind The King's 'death' have lead many fans to believe he is still alive. Now you can track him down with the help of a Priscilla Mask, an instant Elvis Ready Reckoner, 300 amazing Elvis Facts, a 'scoop' of pictures of The King taken since his 'death', cartoons of Elvis in his preferred professions, lists of his favourite meals, cars, girls, etc. And there is a reward of £2 million for the capture of The King. IN COLOUR. *£6.99*

The Beerlover's Bible & Homebar Handbook
(also in the shape of a beercan)
Do you love beer? Then this is the book you've been waiting for - a tantalising brew of fascinating facts to help you enjoy your favourite fluid all the more. Discover how to... serve beer for maximum enjoyment... brew your own beer... cook tasty recipes from beer soup to beer sweets... entertain with beer... But that's not all! With a listing of beers from all over the world, with flavours, colours and potency, you'll become a walking encyclopedia on beer. How better to win round after round by challenging your beer-loving mates in your local. *£3.99*

How to Get Rid of Your Boss
No matter how much you love your work, there is always one person who makes your professional life a misery - your boss. But all that can change. Find out, with the use of helpful diagrams and cartoons, how to get rid of this person that you despise. It's your chance to get your own back and really break free! *£3.99*

The Secret Lives of Teddy Bears
(with a FREE jointed Teddy Bear)
An explanation as to how those annoying little things in life really happen - who hides your keys, who alters your alarm clock and who causes taps to drip. There's also a Teddy Quiz... Bears on Film and Vinyl... Real Life Teddy Bear Facts... Teddy's Timetable... Teddies through History... and a lot more. *£3.99 - with free Teddy.*

MORE HUMOUR TITLES...

A Wunch of Bankers

Do you HATE BANKS? Then you need this collection of stories aimed directly at the crotch of your bank manager. A Wunch of Bankers mixes cartoons and jokes about banks with real-life horror stories of the bare-faced money-grabbing tactics of banks. If you think you've been treated badly, read these stories!!!! *£3.99*

If you would rather not damage your copy of *Fatus Gitosaurus & Friends*, please use plain paper and remember to include all the details listed below!

Please send me a copy of

I enclose a cheque/payment made payable to 'Take That Ltd'. **Postage is free within the U.K.** Please add £1 per title in other EEC countries and £3 elsewhere.

Name:_____

Address:_____

_____

_____

Postcode:_____

Please return to:

Take That Books, P.O.Box 200, Harrogate, HG1 4XB

The Bog Book

(in the shape of a toilet seat)

How much time do you spend in the bog every day? Are you letting valuable time go to waste? Not any longer! Now you can spend every second to your advantage. The Bog Book is packed with enough of the funny, the weird and the wonderful to drive you POTTY. Fill your brain while you empty your bowels... *£3.99*

The Drinker's IQ Test

Have you ever wondered if drink is affecting your brain? Then this book will confirm your worst fears or give you a clean bill of health. Do you know how much pub crisps work out at per tonne? What would you do if a German gave you two-fingers? How much beer can anybody drink on an empty stomach? And while you are thinking, there's a collection of the world's best drinking jokes to relax your brain. *£3.99*

101 Uses for Granny

"I don't want to be a burden" says Granny. Well, now she won't be. With 101 good uses, you'll wonder how you ever got by before. You can use your Granny to... Warn motorists of your long load... Slow down incoming jets... Mark the fact that you've climbed Everest... Welcome your visitors as a talking doormat... Hold your TV ariel in the best position... and if you are ever short of a Guy in November... *£3.99*